MY FRENCH COUNTRY HOME

MY FRENCH COUNTRY HOME

ENTERTAINING THROUGH

THE SEASONS

SHARON SANTONI

PHOTOGRAPHS BY **FRANCK SCHMITT**

GIBBS SMITH
TO ENRICH AND INSPIRE HUMANKIND

Sharon Santoni grew up in England but married a Frenchman and has raised her family in Normandy, France. Her blog, *My French Country Home,* is read daily by thousands all over the world, and her Stylish French Box has many happy subscribers pleased to receive their quarterly box of French goodies. She writes about daily life in rural France; the ups and downs of family life; her inspiring French girlfriends; the intricacies of village life; and her love of searching for brocante treasure in the flea markets of Paris and the countryside.

For my mother,

who always entertained

with ease.

SHARON SANTONI

contents

introduction

In French, entertaining is translated as *l'art de recevoir,* or "the art of receiving." Pretty strange to talk about receiving when, actually, the host is the one doing all of the work and laying out the spread. But perhaps the receiving is in the gift of companionship that comes our way when we entertain—the opportunity to create something delicious, something beautiful and welcoming as well as the pleasure of sharing the moment.

Entertaining in France is a part of everyday living. Casual or formal meals are an intrinsic part of the culture, and as a native English woman, I have learned to love this way of living and blend it with my own upbringing.

Growing up in a big family where the doors were always wide open to relatives and friends, a love of entertaining is in my blood. From my earliest years I have memories of huge meals around long, noisy tables; of small cozy tea parties; of open-house Christmas brunches that lasted all day; and of never-ending dinner parties where good food and lively conversation accompanied us into the small hours of the morning.

When I was little, I loved being at my grandmother's for tea. She was a part of that generation that had time for the little things in life that make such a difference. I always appreciated the care she took in laying out a tea tray, complete with home-baked scones and cakes, little pots of homemade jam, and tiny sandwiches filled with cucumber and salmon dotted with a single flower perched on top . . . just because. Tea was taken in the garden in the summer and around the fire in the winter. And even if it was just the two of us, there was always a pretty tablecloth and a napkin each, and often she'd lay the table with her beautiful best china, because, as she liked to remind me, "there's no point in having it if you don't use it."

My mother was a great entertainer too. I have never equaled her big Sunday lunches, and she was the one who taught me that it's not a big deal to throw a party with food for a huge crowd, providing you think it through and remember to enjoy each minute. When I joined the local youth club in my teens (this was country living, and entertainment was hard to come by) and announced to my mum that it was customary for members of the club to invite the others home for evening coffee and that I'd like to do that and, by the way, there would be over one hundred people coming, she simply replied that she'd probably need to buy some more cups and some extra biscuits.

In short, I grew up sure in the knowledge that there was never a lack of excuses for entertaining friends, and when I came to France as a student, this family background blended with my discovery of French culture.

I've tried to pass this love of entertaining on to our four children, who have long since flown the nest. When they were still small, their birthdays were always fun and often involved ponies, bouncy castles, relay races, treasure hunts and a variety of dressing-up costumes. When the children were still small, birthdays were always a good excuse for a big party. Invitations were homemade, as was the often overly ambitious birthday cake. I remember my just-turned-six-year-old handing out her party invitations outside the school gate and—without consulting me first—announcing to her friends that her birthday cake would be "pink and have six tiers," before turning to me with a confident smile. How could I possibly disappoint her? Six tiers there were. The cake may have been more reminiscent of a certain tower in Pisa than Monsieur Eiffel's construction in Paris, but it was quickly eaten, and none of the pretty little guests noticed the lopsided silhouette. The joy is in the sharing.

Once I lived full time in France, there were always opportunities to invite friends to our table. My husband comes from a long line of great cooks, and by his side I discovered the joy of preparing food, the trips to the farmers market to buy fresh produce, the planning of a menu according to what we found there, as well as the careful matching of the right wine to each dish.

Since in France we live in a climate where the seasons are clearly marked, we have the additional pleasure of there always being something to look forward to. From the change of air in the autumn that makes us long for comfort food again, to winter meals to warm us after a Sunday walk in the forest, to spring spreads created with the first fruits and vegetables of the new season, to summer, when the warm weather allows us to dine alfresco and linger late over a table in the company of good friends.

Living in the countryside keeps us especially aware of the seasons. Our small village is bordered by a forest on one side and crop-growing fields all around. The forest changes color without our help, and the fields are landscaped by local farmers as they plough, sow and harvest. Each fall, when the first new shoots begin to sprout, I am keen to see which crop has been sown in the fields that we can see from our house. Not because it will be produce that we will eat, but because the color and nature of the crop will affect our view and even our mood.

Along our valley we are fortunate to have many beautiful gardens, Spring sees lilacs and wisteria dripping over stone walls and doorways. In June the roses bend low beneath the weight of their blooms, and in the autumn the dahlias explode like fireworks until the first frost signals their retreat.

Tablescapes change with the seasons too. No matter how simple or spontaneous the occasion, I have to lay a few flowers and candles on the table. And if I have the time and the garden is flourishing, then I'll happily go all out and decorate the table from one end to the other, simply because it makes everyone smile. It's not about trying to impress or putting on a show; it's just about living in the present.

As the seasons shift, they dictate how we feel, our dress, our lifestyle down to the food that is on our plates. We savor the privilege of eating fresh, ripe food: from the strawberries that first appear in April to the grapes and mushrooms that flavor our autumn menus.

This book is born from my experience of everyday living in France. I hope that in my tablescapes and flowers you'll find some inspiration for your tables through the seasons, and that, like me, you will also enjoy the simple pleasure of entertaining friends and family. This isn't a cookbook, but I've included a few simple recipes, mostly classics from traditional French cuisine.

Franck Schmitt's beautiful photos were taken at my house and also in the homes of some very patient friends. To each of them I owe a big thank-you, but maybe it would be more appropriate to repay them with a lovely meal and a good bottle of wine . . . *à la française.*

SPRING

pring is long-awaited here in Normandy. By March, we are craving sunshine and keep our eyes closely trained on the trees, hoping to spot the first sign of a tiny new bud, a herald of the season of renewal. And as those buds unfurl and grow, the forest behind the house gradually glows bright green and promises that warmer days are not far away.

I keep a couple of horses at home, so my winters involve a lot of mud and some fairly unglamorous tasks, such as hauling hay and fresh water to the paddocks. After three months of nearly freezing temperatures, I am definitely eager to move on.

The birds provide one of my earliest indicators that a shift is taking place. Over the field where the horses graze, skylarks start singing in late February. High up in the sky, their distinctive warble carries far as the male birds try to impress the girls. Hearing the first lark song of the season announcing the unofficial end of the winter months never fails to make me smile with a tinge of relief.

All through the winter we have been cooped up inside with crackling fires burning in the fireplaces, so from the end of March and onward, any opportunity to get outside is welcome, even if it's only for a quick espresso or with a pair of *secateurs* in hand to start some spring pruning.

The first flowers are the daffodils that grow in loose groups on the lawn and the white petals that open across the branches of the huge magnolia tree, illuminating the garden. Once these are finished blooming, we know that the wisteria will not be far behind. This is the moment to start tidying the garden and planting for the summer months ahead.

Our own *potager* is fairly modest, but our closest neighbors are true experts in the kitchen garden. Even during the chilly afternoons of March, they can be found turning over the rich brown earth and sowing the early onions or the first potatoes. When we first moved into our house, my neighbors, who grow literally one ton of potatoes in their impeccable weed-free *potager,* asked with earnest curiosity what I'd be growing in the way of food for the family. When they understood that I planned to cultivate mostly salads, tomatoes and courgettes, there was a long silence. We did not have the same priorities and I clearly was not going to make the grade. During the following year, their misgivings about my choice of crops never stopped them being generous and friendly, and I'd often find a basket of cherries or beans or potatoes left outside my door.

In spring our local farmers market takes on a very different appearance as well. After months of apples and pears, we begin to see the first strawberries and, of course, the asparagus. Aah, the asparagus! Is it because it's available for so a short a time that we love it so much?

The change from winter to spring inspires us to entertain again. Here in Normandy, we are generally able to eat lunch outside for the first time of the year in March. It may not be truly warm yet, but the pleasure of sitting in the sun is undeniable. Having hosted and been guests indoors all through

In the *potager* I often let the rhubarb shoot to flower, just for the pleasure of seeing their tall white spires, while antique glass cloches are ready to protect young salads from a late frost.

the winter, we now change the menus and lighten the mood. Gone are the stews and heavy sauces, and in come poached fish, fresh strawberries and mixed salads.

But if I have a special affection for springtime, it is for the month of May—most importantly because that is when we moved into this house. I remember the day so clearly; arriving a couple of hours before the moving van and walking through the empty rooms, flinging open windows and shutters, and feeling the warmth enter along with the delicious perfume of the wisteria in full bloom across the facade of the building.

Today that wisteria is even bigger and has to be pruned twice a year if we don't want it to creep right inside the house. It's a natural reminder that the seasons will always move forward, regardless, and it is for us to adapt, keep up and enjoy.

SUNDAY

BREAKFAST

ON THE

TERRACE

Breakfast has always been my favorite meal of the day. In France, contrary to what is usually believed, it isn't always about croissants and fresh bread, especially if you happen to live in the country and the local bakery is too far to walk. In town it is a different affair. There is always a good baker close at hand, or maybe a favorite corner café where you can sit with a coffee and *pain au chocolat* while reading the paper.

I rarely skip breakfast, and if I'm working in Paris, then a chic breakfast meeting is my favorite way to start the day. It takes me just over an hour to drive into town, and I try to group my meetings on one day of the week. When I know the day ahead is fully booked, I love maximizing my time by starting with a breakfast appointment as there is an immediate intimacy created by seeing someone before the day really starts. A hotel restaurant is the ideal setting, but failing that, a big, bustling bistro will do where the waiters know that time is of the essence and the service is rapid and discreet.

While our four children were growing up, breakfast in a household of six was always a pretty busy affair. During the week, we had our eye on the clock to be sure everyone got to school on time, and on the weekend, there was inevitably a Saturday sports competition or event that someone had to attend.

So on Sundays, I often crept out of the house before the family was awake and stole a few hours for myself at a nearby *brocante* fair. The fairs start early, so I could leave the house at around six, shop for antiques during the dawn hours and happily return home in time for breakfast, complete with fresh bread and croissants for all.

Now that my husband and I are empty nesters, the Sunday morning routine has been rediscovered and new rituals installed. There is no rush; if the weather allows, then we lay a table outside. Fresh baguette, crisp newspapers, fruit, and a good pot of coffee. With the inevitable dog at our feet; the day gets off to quite a civilized start.

RED FRUIT TART

MAKES 8 SMALL (4-INCH OR 10CM) TARTS

1 package frozen piecrust, or 8 oz of pastry

2 ¼ cups (18oz, or 500g) of mixed red fruits

1 cup (8oz, or 125g) sugar

FOR THE CRUMBLE TOPPING:

¼ cup (2oz, or 60g) butter

¼ cup (2oz, or 60g) sugar

½ cup (4oz, or 120g) flour

Salt

Preheat oven to 375°F (190°C). Line the individual tart molds with your favorite pie crust dough and bake blind until golden brown.

While these are baking, heat the red fruit and sugar in a small saucepan until softened, but don't let the mixture bubble.

Make the crumble topping by mixing the butter, sugar, and flour with a pinch of salt. Rub lightly between your fingers until it resembles coarse breadcrumbs.

Remove the piecrusts from the oven and spoon enough of the red fruit mixture over the bottoms to half fill the pastry shells.

Top the fruit mixture with a light sprinkling of the crumble and return the tarts to the oven until the crumble is light brown.

Remove from the oven and leave to cool slightly before slipping the tarts from the molds. Serve warm.

A table on the terrace, the garden all around, and fresh croissants to accompany the coffee and newspapers— the rediscovered pleasures of a Sunday morning.

A bundle of antique sheet music, found at a local Sunday-morning *brocante* fair, is ideal to use at the piano or simply for decoration.

LUNCH IN THE GARDEN

I found our house against all odds. We had been renting an orangery in Normandy for a couple of years but were ready to buy our own home. French real estate agents do not share information easily, and before the days of the internet, procuring details of properties for sale was a full-time job!

I faxed or wrote letters to all the local realtors and notaries, but none of them got back to me—until finally, after a couple of months, I received a phone call and heard the hoped-for words. "I may have a property that will interest you." My excitement was only fleeting, because once I was at his office, the realtor insisted on showing me pictures of ugly, tiny houses that bore no resemblance to the details on my wish list.

As chance would have it , he was called out of the room to take an important phone call, and while he was gone I leapt off my chair and grabbed the most interesting looking property file from his desk. Flicking quickly through the pages, I came across a picture of a white house that looked promising. The description confirmed my interest, and when the realtor came back into his office, I showed him the property and told him that I wanted to visit the house.

He looked worried. "I must talk to Monsieur le Directeur," he spattered before disappearing again. Five minutes later he returned with his boss, who explained to me that the house belonged to an important family, and that he wasn't sure that he

should show it to me, especially as my husband wasn't with me! I persuaded them that I was quite capable of visiting a house on my own, and off we went. I spent over an hour looking around the property, and that evening I told my husband that I had seen the house where we should raise our family.

Apparently, though, I had not made the right impression on the real estate agent, and when after a second visit we contacted him with an offer, he refused to take our calls, let alone pass our proposal on to the owners.

By a lucky coincidence, a few weeks later a girlfriend told me she had met some people with a house for sale that may interest me. It was the same property.

The family that owned the house were indeed prominent in France, and also a tad complicated to deal with. It took us two years before the sale was finally closed and we had the keys in our hands.

The day the sale went through, my husband and I drove straight from the notary's office to the house. We turned the big key in the gate and walked around the garden, and then again through the house. With tears of happiness in my eyes, I squeezed his hand and whispered, "We will love living here, and just imagine the parties we'll hold!"

And that is what has happened. Now twenty years later, this house has seen teenagers come of age; large family lunches with four generations around the table; long, late dinners; busy brunches; and whole nonstop weekends of fun! Tables have been laid in the house, down the drive, in the barn and on the lawn. We can always find a reason to celebrate.

This is a house that is made for entertaining. It is not too big, nor pretentious or intimidating, just friendly and welcoming. It is a house that is made to be filled with rowdy family life, dogs, children and friends. A house to love, a house of a lifetime.

Previous overleaf: Laying the table in the center of the lawn requires some to-ing and fro-ing, but guests are always happy to carry a dish or a bottle of wine, and the pleasure of eating surrounded by the garden makes it all worthwhile.

As a last-minute detail before guests arrive, I love to add a sprig or a flower to each plate. The sun isn't too hot in the spring, and these single blooms will hold their own until the end of the meal.

On a long summer table, I often mix embroidered tablecloths and bring the table together with monogrammed napkins bought over the years at local antique fairs.

EASTER BENEATH THE MAGNOLIA

The magnolia tree in our garden is a gentle giant. Majestic and elegant, it spreads its branches in all directions but is limited to the space left available by its neighbors: two centennial holly trees and an oversized cypress that are regularly trimmed to allow the magnolia to express itself fully and easily. Until I lived in a house with a magnolia in the garden, I never knew that it smelled so sweet or that when in flower it could light up the garden like an electric bulb.

When we first moved here, the structure of the garden was very basic. The former owners had used the house as a weekend home for thirty-odd years, and it was all about low maintenance. I let the first year go by, more or less observing what each season revealed, and in February I discovered that most of the beds were dominated by little white snowdrops. That spring I dug up thousands of snowdrops and replanted them all in the lawn beneath the magnolia. Today, they have multiplied to form a pond of white flowers that make a mirror image of the shape of the large tree above. When it is in bloom, the magnolia attracts all the attention, and if the weather permits for us to be outside, it pulls us like a magnet. There we sit, in a garden seat, an easy chair with a newspaper and a coffee, or sometimes even around an Easter table.

Our Easter is all about pastel colors, and the pink-and-white flowers of the magnolia complement the pascal tablescape beneath. The grass around this area, speckled with spring primroses, is the perfect place to hide a few eggs for the hunt. And although it may not be warm enough to spend the whole day outside, a couple of hours at an Easter table, making the most of the first sunshine of the season and the perfume of the flowers, makes for an idyllic spring Sunday.

The natural color of the brown
eggs is a pretty foil to the
primroses and moss gathered
from the garden.

When you're lucky enough to lay your hands on some really exceptional flowers, then it's the moment to produce something spectacular by spreading the shapes and colors among several vases.

Lilacs, viburnums and honeysuckle, arranged on small cake
stands, are set alone on a tea table or in symmetrical form
against a wall.

Our guest cottage is given a big spring clean,

making it ready to welcome friends and family

who arrive for a day or two, or more, then settle

in to make the little house their own.

From antique white tureens to simple milk jugs and earthenware crocks, it's great to vary and not be shy about using receptacles out of context.

May is cherry season here. Bowls of cherries are quickly eaten, and we love cherry preserves or the traditional French dessert of clafoutis.

After our neighbor Odette passed away at the fine age of ninety-eight, her house stood empty for a few years. I kept in contact with the family members, but they lived far away; so the garden, which was once tenderly cared for, was quickly overrun by weeds. I knew how much Odette had loved her garden and will never forget how she often invited my children and me through her gate to pick raspberries, to feed her rabbits, or help ourselves to a glut of apples from her orchard.

So during those years when the house stood empty, I sometimes grabbed a basket and climbed over the garden wall and walked again around her garden, pulling some weeds for her and maybe pruning her favorite rose bush before coming home with a big basketful of ruby-red cherries that would have otherwise been left to the birds.

CHERRY CLAFOUTIS

SERVES 6

A clafoutis is one of the most traditional French desserts, the sort of thing that everyone makes at home. It is usually made with a sort of thick pancake batter, which I used to find a bit boring until I discovered this wonderful recipe with ground almonds added to the mix. Now that's a whole new story!

10 oz (300g) cherries; choose a variety that is sweet but slightly acidic

FOR THE CRÈME D'AMANDES:

1/2 cup (4oz, or 100g) butter

1/2 cup (4oz, or 100g) sugar

1/2 cup (4oz, or 100g) ground almonds

1/2 teaspoon cornstarch

1 egg

FOR THE CRÈME PATISSIÈRE:

3 egg yolks

1 dessertspoon cornstarch

1 heaping cup (8 1/2 fl oz, or 25cl) milk

Preheat the oven to 350°F (180°C). Butter an 11-inch (28cm) earthenware tart mold.

Remove the stems from the cherries, and if you prefer you can stone them too. Most people think it's more polite to stone the cherries, but I leave the stones in and warn guests to be careful; I'm sure the stones add a little extra flavor.

For the clafoutis, make two different preparations: a *crème d'amandes* and a *crème pâtissière*. First, make the *crème d'amandes*. In a mixer, blend the butter to soften well; then add the sugar, ground almonds, and cornstarch. Add the egg and mix thoroughly.

To make the *crème patissière,* beat the egg yolks and cornstarch together in a medium bowl. Bring the milk to the boil and pour into the eggs. Return the milk and egg mixture to the pan and cook gently until it starts to thicken and coats the spoon evenly.

Once the cream is cooked enough, pour it back into the mixing bowl and leave to cool for a few minutes.

Meanwhile, scatter the cherries evenly over the bottom of the buttered tart mold.

Mix the two creams together delicately and pour over the cherries. Pop into the oven for 30 minutes, or until a knife comes out clean.

Remove from the oven and serve warm directly from the tart mold.

Blossoms in the orchards and gardens and canola in the fields means

spring is definitely in full swing.

Linen sheets dried in the sunshine smell sweet and crease less. Before the days of clotheslines, the old linen sheets were spread out on meadow grass to dry, the chlorophyll from the grass drawing the oxygen from the damp fabrics and drying them bright white.

Just beyond our village lives a farmer named Amaury who has a large field turned over to asparagus. From the narrow lane that passes the farm, we see the crop in preparation with soft earth shored up around the delicate spears emerging from the ground. Once the stalks are ready to harvest, Amaury hammers a sign up outside his gate—nothing fancy, just "Asperges." That is all that is needed for his regular clients to start driving through the gate and leaving with the precious vegetable wrapped in neat bundles. If perchance they arrive too late and the day's crop has been sold out, then they reserve a couple of bunches for the next day. For this is the joy of eating local and by season. Nothing can beat the flavor of a crop that has been picked only a few hours before it lands on your plate. There is a tremendous community feeing in buying your food from the person who has produced it and chatting about the weather and if there has been enough rain or sunshine for his crop. It makes the food taste even better.

ASPARAGUS

This recipe is for fresh green asparagus, although the method also works with white asparagus as well.

2 bunches asparagus

1 tablespoon olive oil

Wash the asparagus and remove the lower 2 inches of each stalk. This can either be done with a knife or by simply snapping the stalk, the idea being that the stalk will snap at the point where it becomes tender.

Heat a large spoonful of olive oil in a wide shallow pan and cook gently until it is just beginning to brown. If you are worried about the asparagus not cooking through completely, then you can cover the pan with a lid to increase the heat.

Once the asparagus is completely cooked, slide onto a serving dish and sprinkle with a pinch of coarse sea salt.

Although it may feel like spring, traditional gardeners here will never plant out their tomatoes before the "Saints de Glace" (the Ice Saints) have passed in the middle of May. Until then they are safely protected in a greenhouse or tunnel.

Tinged with pink, the apple blossoms in our local orchards bear the promise of autumn fruit.

SUMMER

A visitor traveling through France during the warmest months quickly understands the importance of the traditionally long French summer break. In small provincial towns, entire streets of stores go quiet for several weeks during the month of August while the owners close up shop to take a rest and enjoy some important family time. Most French people are entitled to five weeks of vacation during the year, and they like to use a large part of their allowance during the summer—visiting family, driving down south, or heading into the mountains, as *il faut changer d'air,* (yes, everyone needs a "change of scenery!").

As there are so many beautiful regions to choose from, many people opt to stay in France for the holidays with the most popular destinations being in the south for the warmth, but also the mountains for hiking, or the center of France, where the weather is reliable and it is less crowded.

Even in Paris the change of mood is tangible: the traffic is lighter, the parking is free and there is a festive mood in the air as café terraces overflow with unhurried clients happy to make a coffee last for an hour and take their time reading the newspaper or eating a light lunch in the sunshine.

During August, we see our friends from Normandy and Paris in Provence or on the Côte d'Azur or in the southwest as we all migrate towards the sun. And, of course, eating well and entertaining during the summer holiday is an important part of the enjoyment to be had. Much pleasure is derived from invitations returned from one region to the next, and the warmer temperatures make for a more relaxed ambiance.

Heading from one end of the country to the other also means that we change our eating habits. Being away from a work routine leaves more time to shop at the local markets and take our time over shared meals. Many regions of France have their own gastronomical specialties. When we are in the south, we make the most of the peaches and melons that cannot be grown in Normandy; their sweet flavors are a delicious part of any summer meal. In the southwest we hunt out local duck farmers, and in Corsica we love the inimitable flavor of the artisan dried meats and hams.

But when in Normandy, my favorite summer month is June, when the roses are at their best and the garden becomes the perfect backdrop for al fresco meals—from long lunches on the lawn to dinners around the barbecue. The flower beds that are overflowing with color and the house dressed in its heavy façade of wisteria leaves not only create a pretty setting but also supply all the flowers that I need for my tablescapes. Whether I decorate the table with a line of single buds in tiny liqueur glasses or with a larger, more elaborate arrangement, during this season more than any other I love to have the house filled with vases and pots of blooms from the garden.

The days are long and the evenings stretch far beyond their normal time frame as we sit down to a meal later than usual and enjoy dinners with friends until well after midnight. We are fortunate not to be bothered by bugs, and the windows on the house are flung wide open for weeks on end.

Our vegetable garden is busy producing salads, radishes and maybe the first *mangetout* (snow peas). Strawberries growing in pots on the terrace are mostly eaten with breakfast. All quick additions to summer meals that taste so much more delicious for having just been picked.

Summer is, more than any other season, the moment for spontaneous last-minute invitations. The promise of a warm evening is more than enough reason to make a few phone calls; friends turn up for dinner or for drinks served with small *amuse-bouches* at the end of the day.

What is meant to be a time for rest can quickly become a social whirlwind, with dinners, apéritifs and lunches slotted into the diary. An afternoon siesta can become mandatory, and maybe this is why in France we have the reputation of taking our time: we have a sense of priorities and balance is key. Work is important, but so is family; partying is fun, but you need to rest; good food is primordial but in moderation.

Above all other seasons, summer in France epitomizes the way that many people see the country. Indelibly linked to the image of being on holiday, it is all about eating well, soaking up the sunshine, savoring every minute of each day and storing new energy for the autumn ahead.

It's fun to make a statement with flowers on the table and a decorative leaf on each place. The tall blooms can be moved to the ends of the table when the meal commences, but in the meantime, the colorful rustic jugs are a nice contrast to antique crystal and cut glass.

PICNIC BY THE RIVER

There is something festive about a picnic, as if the simple fact of packing food into a basket and choosing to sit on a blanket laid on the ground rather than on a comfortable chair around a table is enough to make the meal feel special.

I have always loved a good picnic. Never mind the temperature: it's the mood that counts. When I was young, it was a family tradition on New Year's Day to pack our meal and either head to the sea or to a beautiful racetrack in the south of England, where in between sandwiches we would lay small bets on the horses. It was cold; it was winter; but it didn't matter—it was fun. The awareness that it wasn't reasonable or normal to be picnicking in close-to-freezing temperatures merely added to our enjoyment.

I continued this habit with my own children. On school days, rather than leave them all at the school cafeteria or attempt to drive them home for a rushed meal before afternoon lessons, I far preferred to pack a picnic and take them all to a nearby park, where they ate their lunch while hanging upside down from climbing frames or whirling around on roller skates. Perhaps not ideal for digestion, but great for letting off steam.

Picnics work well for all generations. Old and young can fish together, canoe, or simply chat. The meal can be prepared by one or by many. It is an opportunity to get away from your routine, from commitments and hopefully from phones. Lounging in the shade on a blanket beside a slow-moving river is far more conducive to good conversation than a table in a noisy restaurant. Food should be delicious but not complicated: sandwiches, quiches, fruit tarts— all easy to hold while getting on with the more important business of catching a trout or painting.

Above all, a picnic should never be hurried.

QUICHE LORRAINE

Use your favorite savory pastry to line a tart mold, preferably one with a loose base. I like to use a mold that is about 10 inches (25 cm) in diameter.

1 pastry crust

7 ounces (200g) sliced bacon of your choice

5 eggs

1 scant cup (20cl, or 7fl oz) cream

Salt and pepper

1 cup (3oz, or 85g) grated cheese such as cheddar or French Emmental

Line the tart mold with the pastry and cover the pastry in waxed paper. Sprinkle a few dried beans over the paper and pop the pastry into a preheated 375°F (190°C) oven to bake blind. After 10 minutes, remove the waxed paper and bake for another 5 minutes, until the pastry is just beginning to turn golden.

Meanwhile, heat the chopped bacon in a pan until it starts to crisp; drain off the fat.

In a bowl, mix the eggs with the cream; season lightly with salt and pepper to taste. To this mixture add most of the grated cheese and beat well.

Remove the pastry from the oven, sprinkle the bacon pieces over the bottom then gently pour in the cream and egg mix. Those who love cheese can sprinkle a little extra grated cheese over the top of the tart.

Place the quiche in the oven; it will be ready in about 20 minutes, or when a knife inserted into the quiche comes out clean. Can be served warm or cold. Excellent for picnics by the river!

What could be more luxurious than an afternoon spent by the river with good food, good friends and a glass of wine, painting, fishing, reading or maybe dozing in the shade.

There is a trout farm along the valley, and quite a few trout seem to find their way along this stream. We rarely catch anything, but the pleasure is in the waiting.

STRAWBERRY TART

MAKES ONE 9-INCH TART

To make a perfect strawberry tart that will keep its shape when taken on a picnic, you will need a good piecrust that behaves properly once unmolded. I love to use an almond pastry crust for this recipe: the flavor of the almonds complements the strawberries, and the crust is rich and delicious. Providing you allow this pastry some time to rest, this is an amazingly simple recipe.

FOR THE PASTRY CRUST:

1 1/2 cups (7oz, or 200g) all-purpose flour

1 1/2 cups (6oz, or 175g) ground almonds

1 cup (8oz, or 175g) sugar

1 cup (7oz, or 200g) cold butter, diced

1 egg yolk

FOR THE CREAM:

2 cups (1/2 liter) milk

1 vanilla pod, slit lengthwise into two parts

4 egg yolks

1/2 cup (4oz, or 100g) sugar

1/3 cup (1 1/2oz, or 40g) cornstarch

Marsala wine, optional

3/4 pound (300g) strawberries

3 large spoonfuls red currant jelly

FOR THE PASTRY CRUST:

Place all the ingredients, except for the egg yolk, into a food processor and blend until the texture looks like breadcrumbs. Add the egg yolk and blend again until the pastry comes together as a soft dough.

It is best to us a loose-based tart mold for this recipe, and also line the base with a circle of waxed paper to make it easier to slide the finished tart onto the serving dish. Because this is such a rich pastry, it is almost impossible to roll. The answer is to gently press the pastry into the base, being sure to bring the crust up around the edges until it just overlaps the top of the mold. The crust should be an even thickness all over.

Cover the crust bottom with a second piece of waxed paper, and pour in baking beans to bake blind. Bake for about 20 minutes at 375°F (190°C) until the edges of the pastry start to turn golden; then remove the paper and beans and bake for another 5 to 10 minutes, until the bottom is a beautiful, evenly cooked biscuit. Set aside to cool completely.

FOR THE CREAM:

Heat the milk in a pan with the vanilla pod.

In a bowl, beat the egg yolks with the sugar then add the cornstarch. Pour the hot milk into the egg-sugar mixture and mix well. Return mixture to the pan and cook gently, stirring constantly, for about 4 minutes, until the cream thickens. Remove the vanilla pod and pour the cream back into the bowl to cool down.

I like to add a spoonful of almond-flavored Marsala wine to 1/4 cup (60ml) of the cream and beat until thick. But be careful: your cream will be more liquid once you do this. So if you are worried about perfect presentation, then it would be safer to omit this step.

Once the cream is completely cold, spoon it into the pastry crust, and arrange the strawberries, whole or in halves, to cover the cream completely. Heat the red currant jelly in a pan and carefully pour it over the strawberries, trying not to let it overflow. Chill in the fridge before serving.

STRAWBERRY JAM

MAKES 4 TO 5 MEDIUM-SIZED JARS

My idea of summer in a jar!

2 pounds (1 kg) strawberries, hulled

3 ³/4 cups (750g) sugar

Juice of 1 lemon

Wash and warm your jelly jars so they are squeaky clean and preferably warm. I always run my jars through the dishwasher so they are dry and warm as I finish the jam making.

Clean the strawberries with a piece of paper towel rather than adding excess water by washing them. Put the berries, either whole or halved, into a big stoneware bowl with the sugar. Toss the fruit gently so the sugar is evenly distributed. Cover the bowl and leave overnight. This process helps the fruit maintain its shape rather than dissolving, but if you prefer your jam to have a smoother texture, you can skip this step.

Pop a couple of saucers into the freezer; you'll need them for testing the jam as it cooks.

Pour the fruit and sugar into a large nonreactive pan; add the lemon juice. Warm gently until all the sugar is dissolved then turn up the heat and get the jam bubbling. Boil hard for about 10 minutes then turn off the heat. Stir occasionally to ensure even cooking. Test the jam by putting a spoonful on one of the saucers and, after a few seconds, pushing gently with your finger. If the jam surface crinkles, then the jam is ready; if not, then cook for 3 minutes more and test again on the second saucer.

Once the jam is ready, turn off the heat. Remove any scum from the surface of the jam. Leave to settle for about 20 minutes then ladle hot jam into the warm jars. Process in a hot water bath according to safe canning procedures.

PREDINNER

DRINKS

The aperitif, or predinner drink, is a large part of French culture and entertaining. Whether we go out for a meal, eat at a friend's house or at home, an evening will always be preceded by the aperitif. This is one of the reasons why dinner is a long event. It would be unheard of to arrive and be taken straight to the table.

Generally a dinner invitation is for 8:30 pm, and guests are offered something to drink with a few snacks to eat at the same time. The drinks can be martinis, cocktails or aniseed-flavored Pastis in the south, but most often champagne is the favorite. A kir is white wine served with a little red fruit cordial in the base of the glass, and a kir royale is the same thing but uses champagne instead of wine.

The snacks might simply be small pieces of a savory bread with a cheese or avocado spread or maybe a bowl of olives. In the winter we serve slices of hot sausage or warm *gougères* (cheese puffs), and in the summer the bread is often replaced by sticks of raw cucumber, or tiny pink radishes, washed and trimmed, ready to dip into hummus or tarama (spread made from fish roe).

The purpose of this interlude before the meal is to open the appetite and break the ice between guests, who have all come from their busy day and routine. Glasses are filled several times over and guests help themselves to the appetizers, but of course, they bear in mind that they are about to move over to the dining table, where they will most likely be offered a three- or four-course meal punctuated by cheese and salad.

Sometimes, because the aperitif is such an enjoyable moment and so very easy to put together, an invitation is just for drinks. In this case, the time will be set a little earlier, with drinks served from around 7:00 to 9:00 or maybe 10:00, when guests return home and those who are still hungry can have a meal there.

Regardless of the time, this particular moment of the day is a wonderful shared pleasure at any time of year.

To create a pretty bouquet that runs the length of a table, the easiest way is to use multiple small containers and short stems. Here roses and hydrangeas fill more than a dozen glass cups.

ROSE PETAL JELLY

MAKES 2 (8-OUNCE, OR 500ML) JARS

Few jams or jellies could be as evocative and wildly perfumed as rose jelly. We have a lot of roses in the garden, and since we don't spray them with chemicals, I love to use their petals for making jelly. It's best to use the most perfumed roses, and the darker colored flowers will produce a deeper colored jelly.

Petals from 8 large rose heads

2 overflowing cups (17fl oz or 500 ml) water

2 heaping cups (17oz or 500g) sugar

Juice of 1 lemon

Place 2 saucers in the freezer; you'll need them for checking the jelly as it cooks.

Check the rose petals for any insects when you remove them from their stalks. Then drop the petals into a large saucepan with the water. Sometimes I let them stand for a while to infuse, but that's just a question of time management.

Bring the rose petals and water to a simmer, and allow to simmer for about 5 minutes. I prefer not to have too many petals in my jelly, so at this point I strain the petals and press them in a sieve to extract as much perfume as possible.

Return the petal-free liquid to the pan, and add the sugar and lemon juice. Heat slowly until the sugar is dissolved, and then turn up the heat and allow to boil for about 4 minutes. Turn off the heat. Test the jelly for setting by putting a spoonful on one of the saucers and, after a few seconds, pushing gently with your finger. If the jelly surface crinkles, it is ready; if not, then cook for 3 minutes more and test again on the second saucer.

If you like to see a few rose petals in the jars of jelly, and that is a pretty sight, then add a handful of fresh, clean petals to the mix while it is still boiling. They will wilt quite quickly but retain their shape and flavor.

Pour the hot jelly into hot jars and seal according to safe canning procedures.

Pannacotta with a fruit coulis makes a simple and light dessert.

Enjoying predinner drinks
in the garden of friends.

It's important to move garden seating to fit the mood and the time of day. Stick to the shade and always seek out the best views.

FOUGASSE BREAD

MAKES 1 FOUGASSE LOAF

Fougasse is a bread that is traditionally made in the south of France but is popular in other areas, often served with wine as an aperitif before dinner. Fougasse can be made as a plain bread or flavored in different savors. This is my favorite, Fougasse aux Olives.

2 cups (9oz, or 250g) white bread flour

1 packet instant yeast

1 teaspoon fine salt

2 tablespoons of olive oil, plus more for drizzling

3/4 cup (6oz, or 170ml) warm water

1 handful pitted black olives, preferably from southern France, halved or roughly chopped

1/2 teaspoon chopped fresh rosemary leaves, optional

Sea salt

If you are kneading by hand, in a large earthenware bowl mix the flour, yeast, and salt. Add the olive oil and stir. Then add the water little by little. If you are using a mixer with a dough hook, use the mixer bowl and allow the machine to knead for about 10 minutes. Either way, you want to end up with a well-mixed, elastic dough that comes away from the sides of the bowl. Near the end of the kneading time, add the olives and, if you wish, you can add a few chopped rosemary leaves at this point.

Grease a deep glass bowl and place the dough in it to rise; set it somewhere warm for about 1 hour, or until the dough has doubled in size.

Use a handful of flour to dust a wooden board. Lift the dough from the bowl. Roll it lightly in the flour then lift onto your baking sheet. Push the dough into a fairly flat oval shape and cut diagonal lines, like the veins of a leaf, on both sides of the center of the dough.

Cover the dough with waxed paper and a clean tea towel; set in a warm place to rise again for about 20 minutes. Preheat the oven to 425°F (220°C).

Drizzle a little olive oil over the dough and sprinkle some good-quality sea salt. Bake for about 20 minutes. This delicious bread can be eaten warm or cold.

BARBECUE WITH ROSES

Our property is not enormous, but as is often the case with old French houses, we are lucky to have several old stone buildings in the garden. A former bread oven has been converted to a guest cottage, a pig sty is now a tool shed, the cow barn is ideal for parties, and the lean-to shelter tacked on to the end of the barn has become our place to cook outdoors.

My husband built the barbecue and even the table and benches, specifically designed to fit as many friends as possible, tucked away around the fire and sheltered from the cool night air. The long, narrow table looks great laid for a meal, whether it be a simple lunch with a girlfriend or a dinner with flowers and the full works.

At the height of summer it isn't dark until 10:00, and we welcome the warm evenings. Typically, a dinner will commence when guests arrive around 8:30. Drinks and appetizers are served for an hour or more, and then we sit down to eat just as it darkness falls. Good food, good company and good wine. Simple pleasures.

The beauty of having a covered barbecue area is that the fire is as much about warming the atmosphere as cooking the meal. If the air is damp and guests start feeling a chill after midnight, then we throw more logs onto the fire, distribute a couple of shawls and let the evening carry on for as long as people are happy to chat.

There is something about this enclosed, covered space that feels intimate and special. The fire at one end of the table throws a pretty light and candles do the rest. Sometimes we have quiet music in the background, and on other occasions lively conversation is all that is needed to keep everyone happy.

Over the years, our grown-up dinner parties and family meals have often morphed into an inclusive gathering with the children inviting friends of their own. My husband taught his sons how to cook over flames, and today they are each comfortable grilling for a crowd. I like to think that beyond simply handling a barbecue grill, we have also handed down the innate pleasure of entertaining.

Sunflowers and summer fruit: vitamins for our body and food for our soul.

AUTUMN

I have discovered that autumn is a special moment for me, a comfort zone, and the season to relax. Summer is often busy with entertaining, being entertained, maintaining the garden and traveling. The holiday months can easily leave you feeling like you need another holiday!

Autumn rolls in with its misty mornings and colder nights. We turn back the clocks and gain an extra hour. We start to think about the end-of-the-year festivities, but as yet there is no urgency. The colors and smells of the season are very evocative: tendrils of smoke from chimneys; mushrooms and damp leaves in the forest; the perfume of ripe apples—they all speak to me and urge me to slow down and simply be present.

This is the season for an easier wardrobe too. Gone is the summer selection of flimsy, lightweight clothes; gone too are the high heels to accompany the pretty dress, or the need to maintain a perfect tan. With the first chill comes the desire to retrieve the cashmere from the back of the wardrobe, to find that hat, to pull out the leather boots and relax into a completely different silhouette.

The garden needs a little cutting back, but putting the borders to bed can wait. This is when I like to take stock of what worked best, what should be moved next spring or duplicated, but also to plan and to hope, to build an expectation of what next year's garden may look like.

Local apples and pears are ripe in September. Some varieties are best to eat straight away, while others can be stored for the winter months.

Entertaining continues but on a more intimate, more cozy level. Catching up with friends over small dinners for four. Romantic evenings in front of the fire. Spontaneous lunches with friends where everyone pitches in. Even if there is the occasional reason to host a bigger lunch or a more fancy dinner, on the whole these months are our moment to take everything a little easier.

We light our first log fires and their flickering flames are a welcome sight, taking the chill out of the end of the day. This is when we restock our log pile in provision for the cooler weather.

Just like the forest animals who stash away a winter supply of food, we store apples and pears from the garden on fruit racks in the cellar and visit a couple of wine producers in Burgundy or farther south. They have completed the harvest, and I love to hear about the year's production while buying wines to replenish the cellar for the years to come.

My autumn entertaining also takes a different form in September, when I host my annual *brocante* tour; guests from all over the world join me in Normandy to hunt for antiques and treasures to take home. Together we explore this lovely corner of France and also visit my very favorite antique fair in Chatou, on the west of Paris. Chatou seems to epitomize and launch the autumn brocante season, especially when we are lucky with the weather and the whole fair is bathed in golden warm sunshine. We spend a day wandering around the fair, looking at paintings, jewelry, textiles and furniture. Lunch is the ideal moment to share what we have bought or would like to buy, and by the end of the day we head back to Normandy happy, with the car packed full of our finds.

Friends abroad often tell me how fortunate we are in France to have more time to enjoy the little things in life. In autumn I think that they are right; it is a happy, fragrant season to be relished, something which is always better when with friends.

Pears are harvested and stacked in wooden crates, ready for the farmers markets.

APPLE TARTE TATIN

MAKES 1 (10-INCH, OR 25CM) TART

An upside down apple tart, or tarte tatin, is a wonderful indulgence, to be enjoyed in the autumn when the apples are being harvested and the nights are drawing in. This is comfort food steeped in tradition.

Be sure to use an apple variety that has plenty of flavor but will also maintain a good shape during cooking. I speak from experience: the first tarte tatin that I ever made, I used an apple that was ideal for purée but not for tarts, and the final result was not at all presentable!

8 apples (choose a variety that will retain its shape in cooking)

½ cup (3 ½oz, or 100g) butter

½ cup (3 ½oz, or 100g) sugar

1 pie crust

Whipped cream or ice cream, optional for serving

To make this recipe I use a heavy-bottomed frying pan that lost its handle many moons ago, which allows me to start cooking the fruit over the heat and then transfer it to the oven to bake the pastry.

Halve, core, and peel the apples.

Melt the butter in a heavy-bottomed pan on low heat and swirl it around. Add the sugar then carefully position the apple halves core side down. Turn up the heat to medium and let the apples cook gently in the butter and sugar with little interference; remember, you want to keep their shape intact. Just be sure to keep moving the pan around on the heat so that the butter and sugar caramelize equally in the pan without getting too dark. After about 10 minutes, gently use a fork and a large spoon to flip the apple pieces so that you now can see the center of the apples.

Cook for another 5 minutes then turn off the heat. Roll out the pastry wide enough to cover the pan, and carefully position it over the fruit. Tuck the pastry into the edges of the pan like a blanket and cut off any excess.

Preheat the oven to 425°F (215°C). Pop the tart into the oven and bake for about 20 minutes, or until golden. Remove from the oven and leave to cool a little before laying a large plate on top of the pastry and gently turning the plate and the tart pan upside down. Set the plate on a table and ease the pan upwards; your fruit should remain in place on the pastry base, but if a piece of fruit remains stuck to the pan, simply slide it back into place with a knife. When the tart is turned upside down, the juices from the fruit soak into the pastry crust.

Serve warm, with or without cream or ice cream.

A TABLE IN THE FOREST

Sometimes you need to do something special, something out of the ordinary—not because there is an important reason or because you are bored or have anything to celebrate, but just because making an exceptional moment out of unexceptional circumstances creates a buzz that is greater than if you had paid the most expensive event organizers in the world.

Taking a table to the forest is a perfect example. It requires some time and effort; it is better with a little forethought and planning, although last minute and spontaneous can work very well too, and in no time, with a couple of helping hands you find yourself with a table of happy friends who sink right into the moment and while away an afternoon with good conversation and delicious food.

It is so calming to be surrounded by tall trees and ferns, and if the table décor reflects the natural décor all around, then it feels even better.

Here in Normandy we are fortunate to have so many forest paths that are open to the public, but they are rarely busy. At most we may see a horse rider or a family walking their dog, or in the autumn a few mushroom hunters, their baskets full of delicious *cèpes* (porcinis) or chanterelles.

An extraordinary setting doesn't require a complicated meal. Seasonal dishes are the most appropriate, and with a little ingenuity, it's even possible to serve warm soup or stew accompanied by a good wine and a great selection of cheese.

Walking the dogs in the forest is a pleasure at any time of year, but the autumn colors make everything more beautiful.

Although it is customary to create a *plateau du fromage,* or cheese board, with a wide variety of cheeses, sometimes we like to choose only goat cheeses, each one different in size, shape and flavor, according to where the goats have been grazing and how their milk has been treated. Here cheeses are unpasteurized, full of flavor. Our favorite is made with milk infused with thyme—it's wonderful!

And at the end of the afternoon, as the temperature drops, we dismantle this ephemeral scene, leaving nothing behind except the occasional crumb for a forest mouse or squirrel. The enjoyment is heightened by the sure knowledge that it was a one-time performance, a fleeting moment that can never be repeated identically.

A few flowers from the garden add to the pleasure of the forest table and make the event feel more festive.

PUMPKIN SOUP

How I love a good vegetable soup—so versatile, so adaptable to what you have in the garden or the fridge, and easy and simple to make. Many vegetable soups are made by cooking the vegetables in water or stock, but for pumpkin soup I prefer to roast the pumpkin and other vegetables in the oven before blending. This method gives a more hearty, slightly caramelized flavor to the vegetables.

No two batches of soup will ever be the same. Not only because the varieties of vegetables themselves can vary in flavor, but also because proportions change according to the size of the vegetables in question.

2 small pumpkins or 1 quarter of a large pumpkin

2 red onions

2 ribs celery

2 cloves garlic

3 cups cherry tomatoes, or 5 slicing tomatoes

Olive oil

Sea salt

Chicken or vegetable stock

Milk, as desired to thin

Salt and pepper

This is how my pumpkin soup generally goes: Wash and cut pumpkin into cubes. (It was a revelation to me a few years ago to learn that I didn't need to remove the pumpkin skin. Our pumpkins are grown organically, so there is no worry about eating the skin.)

Peel and chop the onions, slice the celery, and crush the garlic. Scatter these over a baking tray with the cubed pumpkin. Add the tomatoes and drizzle liberally with a good olive oil; sprinkle with sea salt.

Place the baking tray in the oven at 400°F (200°C) for at least an hour, taking a look now and again to stir the vegetables and be sure they are cooking evenly. Once everything is cooked thoroughly, remove the baking tray from the oven, leave to cool slightly, and then slide batches of the vegetables into a blender. Each batch of blended vegetables can be poured into a saucepan, and when all the vegetables are done, add some stock and some milk to the vegetables until you have the desired thickness for the soup. Add salt and pepper to taste.

Fervent mushroom hunters have their favorite spots in the forest and they keep them

secret. Mushrooms are cut with a knife or snapped at the stem, and if in doubt, the

local pharmacy will always help with identifying the good from the bad.

MUSHROOM BAKE

SERVES 6 TO 8

For this recipe I use a filo or flaky pastry bought from my local baker.

1 puff pastry, or use filo dough

1 ounce (400g) mushrooms

2 cloves garlic

1 shallot, chopped

Olive oil

Generous 1/2 cup (4 fl oz, or 15cl) cream

Salt and pepper

1 egg beaten with 1 tablespoon water

Preheat the oven to 400°F (200°C).

Roll out the pastry into a square approximately 12 inches (30cm) wide, and place on a baking sheet lined with parchment paper. If you want to plait the top of the pastry bake, then draw two light lines on the pastry so that it is visually divided into three equal parts. Using a knife, cut diagonal slits into the two outer thirds of the pastry. This is to form the strips that you will fold to the top and plait together later on.

Clean and slice the mushrooms. Crush the garlic and cook gently in a pan with the shallot and a little olive oil. Add the sliced mushrooms and cook over medium heat until the mushrooms smell divine and any liquid has evaporated. Add the cream, salt and pepper to taste, and cook lightly until the cream has evaporated a little.

Spoon the mushroom mix onto the center third part of the pastry, and bring the strips over, alternating from one side then from the other to form the pastry plait over the mushrooms. Seal the ends of the pastry using a little milk to help the pastry stick together, and coat the entire plait with the beaten egg wash.

Pop it into the oven and bake for around 25 minutes, until golden brown. Serve warm as a snack or to accompany a meat.

FIRESIDE COOKING

Before I came to France, I had never eaten a meal cooked over a fire before. (As a marshmallow grilled on a stick around a campfire simply doesn't count.) I mean a real meal, prepared with care and savored with friends.

There are restaurants in this part of France that specialize in cooking their meats over an open fire. Tender meat is grilled to perfection in front of attentive clients; at home you need a sure hand to do the same.

While at first this may seem ambitious, it really is part of an age-old tradition. The principle of cooking over a fire indoors is not that much different from a barbeque outdoors, but you need the right equipment. Long-handled frying pans, simple open grills or deeper pots are all useful, but the most important item is the support that allows you to raise or lower the food above the fire. You are looking to achieve constant, measured heat rather than carbonizing flames!

We have two open fireplaces in our house, and we cook in either of them, depending on the occasion. The smaller fireplace in the living room may be used to prepare a sausage, cut to share as an appetizer, while the one in the dining room, which is bigger and easier to access, is often used for family meals, with everyone keeping an eye on the food while the table is laid and the rest of the meal prepared.

Lighting a fire always warms up the atmosphere, even if the house is heated. There is a coziness about sitting in front of a fire that nothing else can match. When the flames are also used to prepare the meal, then the feel-good element is only amplified.

Most often we cook a length of sausage coiled up on the grill. Duck confit works well too, with the meat cooking on one level while the accompanying potatoes sizzle in a deeper pan to one side. But the most spectacular meal I have ever seen cooked over a fire was a truffle omelette. Invited to dinner by friends who are both professional chefs, we knew we were in for a treat. They welcomed us to their home deep in the Normandy countryside, and while we shared a glass or two of champagne before the meal, a large bowl was passed from one family member to the next, as the eggs were beaten and beaten, until the result was a light, frothy mix to which they added a small quantity of grated truffle. The eggs were poured into a long-handled frying pan and cooked over the fire, the unique perfume of truffles making our mouths water. A few minutes later, we each had a slice of the truffle omelette on our warmed plates and the room went quiet. It was simply divine!

In our house, my husband and sons enjoy managing the fire, but if I'm on my own at home, I'll happily light one just for me. A winter evening in front of flickering flames with a good book and a sleepy dog . . . what else could I possibly need?

Teatime with friends, sharing small apricot pastries from the local boulangerie.

The mantel over a fireplace is a good place to display a few simple flowers or works of art.

SHOPPING AT THE MARKET

Buying at the farmers market here is so much more than simply ticking off items from a shopping list. Each town has its set market days, sometimes twice a week, and the same vendors can be found at different markets throughout the region. When I go to market, I'm taking part in the local social life. While buying a chicken to roast, I chat with a neighbor about the best way to prepare it. As I pick out a kilo of apples, I hear how the grower was worried about the recent hailstorm that threatened to wipe out his crop. There is little point in trying to shop quickly while there, as the vendors are friendly and love to chat. I expect to meet friends and neighbors and always allow for time to stop and catch up on recent news.

My husband actually shops at the farmers market as much as I do because he loves to cook, and to eat well you need to choose your ingredients with care. There are a couple of good local markets a short drive from our home, and as a long-standing client of them both, he also has his favorite vendors.

When I came from Britain to live in France all those years ago, he was the one who taught me how to shop at the market and that you never go with a set idea or list in mind. Inspiration must come on the spot, surrounded by the sounds and smells and visuals of a well-stocked display. I may arrive at the market planning to buy a chicken, but if I discover that my favorite fishmonger has some beautiful monkfish or that scallops are in season, then the menu will change accordingly.

The market is full of interesting personalities. One man sells only apples in the autumn and winter then strawberries in spring and summer. He produces all the fruit that he sells and he knows everything there is to know about varieties of apples or the effect of rain on red fruit. His stall is a simple trestle table stacked with crates of fruit topped with handwritten sign displaying the prices per kilo. There is always a line of customers and he generally sells out within a couple of hours.

Buying all of your food at the market is locavore heaven. While the producers sell at the market to earn a living, unloading goods several times a week at different markets takes true dedication. I remember once waiting to be served some cream and freshly made butter by one of the local dairy farmers. The cream is ladled from a huge earthenware bowl into small pots that are sealed down, and the butter is cut with a wire from a big slab then wrapped in a paper with the producer's name printed on the outside. That day it was taking longer than usual because he and his wife were explaining to every single client that they would be absent the following week. "It's the first time in twenty-five years," they said apologetically, "but we can't help it—our son is getting married!"

Market stands come in all sizes, from the local vegetable farmer—with his twin sons who we have watched grow up—who arrives with a team of five or six to sell seasonal vegetables and salads. Or at the other end of the spectrum, there is the more elderly lady who takes the precaution of bringing a chair with her to the market and sits down beside her wares: a basket of eggs, a couple of chickens, two crates of apples or a few small baskets of raspberries. I love that sometimes she'll sell flowers from her garden too—bunches of lupins in the summer and zinnias and dahlias in the fall.

Clients move slowly from one stand to the next, with a basket in hand and often a dog by their side. Once their baskets are full,

there is always time for a coffee or lunch at the nearest little café, or to stop at the baker's to buy a baguette, slipped into the basket besides the vegetables.

Above and beyond all of the quaintness and authenticity, I am grateful for the privilege of buying fresh food from reliable producers, of living with the seasons, and of being able to create menus from scratch inspired by whatever is at its best on each particular market day.

It's not unusual to see fruit and vegetables cut open to smell or taste before buying. Choosing the right produce is a serious business!

The garden takes on a relaxed and slightly disheveled air as we move through the autumn. Dahlias, hydrangeas and sedums provide gentle color until the first frosts.

I try to grow many different varieties of dahlias, a staple ingredient for all my autumn bouquets.

Cutting flowers for bouquets becomes a pleasure in its own right as they gradually fill the basket. With stems about ten inches long, they keep each other in place as the basket moves from one bed to the next.

Autumn sunshine catches on the colors of a long table laid

across the center of the garden.

Home-dyed linen sheeting makes beautiful tablecloths and napkins that reflect the colors of the autumn leaves.

WINTER

Just when we are enjoying the last of the autumn color along our valley, winter arrives and catches us off guard with temperatures approaching freezing. On the first morning when the curtains are opened to reveal that the overnight chill has dressed the garden in white, we know that the time has come to wear an extra layer and start thinking about our preparations for the holiday season.

Mornings are cold and crisp as the garden sparkles with frozen leaves and the grass crunches beneath our feet. Just a few weeks earlier, during the last days of autumn, I put the garden to bed, because winter requires clean-cut lines and well-defined shapes in the borders so they look tidy when seen from the house. For the next few months the garden requires no attention, and with the low temperatures, that suits us rather well.

During this time we are pleased to have two open fireplaces in the house, and during the weekends they both burn all day long; mirrored images from one room to the next that are as much about cheering our spirits as raising the temperatures. Baskets of logs are kept well stocked at all times, and everyone keeps an eye on the fires as they walk past, pushing a branch back into place or throwing a new log onto the embers. And if I have time to sit down beside the fire with a book and a cup of coffee, I'm never alone for long, as the fireplace hearth is a favorite place for the dogs too.

November is the time for the occasional quiet dinner with friends, but our minds are already on the entertaining that surrounds Christmas and the New Year. I love the holidays. When the children were little, the house was buzzing with their excitement, and now that they have flown the nest, it's me who gets excited about preparing the house for their return visits. I always buy my tree, or *sapin de Noël,* in early December from a local farm where they patiently let me size up several large trees before making my choice. With help from my husband, we set up the tree in the sitting room, and the distinctive pine perfume accompanied by the twinkle of the lights are the first hints that Christmas is near.

There is a feeling of anticipation in the air that even the dogs can sense. Our smallest dog, Ghetto, who loves to be where the action is, worked out long ago that wrapping up presents is a sign of something good about to happen, and I have to keep the door firmly locked on any half-wrapped gifts.

Once the house is decorated, it's always fun to invite friends over. For many years, we held an open-house brunch in mid-December, with friends coming and going all day long and a never-ending feast laid out on the dining room table. The food was a mix of my British culture and my husband's French traditions. It involved a lot of preparation, but the result made it all worthwhile, and the relaxed atmosphere produced by good food and wine dissipated any hint of hostess stress.

The French celebrations are very different from the Christmas carols and plum pudding that I grew up with in England, but along our valley, there are others who like to mix cultures together during the festive season. In a nearby village, my English girlfriend Bernadette organizes a Christmas carol service each year. Her entire village comes together to sing a mix of English and French hymns, while the village school children act out a nativity play, complete with a donkey, in the nave of the beautiful fourteenth-century church.

In France, Christmas is traditionally more about the family dinner on December 24th than the festivities of the 25th. So in our house we celebrate both. Sometimes friends join us; other times it is just the family and the dogs. The Christmas Eve dinner is carefully chosen to include seasonal specialties such as oysters and foie gras. Champagne and wine accompany the meal, but we wait until the next day to exchange gifts,

pull British crackers and roast the turkey or a goose. After Christmas lunch everyone dons scarves and boots, and we head off for a walk in the forest before coming home to a quiet evening in front of the fire.

In Normandy we don't get much snow, although we have had the occasional white Christmas—just enough snow to last for a couple of days. Any more than a few inches is enough to shut the valley down. We are simply not equipped, and the occasional heavy snowfall often means extra days off from school for the children as classes are closed and school buses stop running.

The remaining weeks of winter after the holidays are the time when we have to pace ourselves, allowing for some extra comfort food and quiet entertaining with close friends. Days are short, nights are long, and after the rush of the end-of-year celebrations, everyone seems to take pleasure in a slow moment before spring comes back to wake us up and fill our days with urgency.

CHRISTMAS

IN RED

My very first experience of a large family gathering in France was a New Year's Eve dinner. Eric, my future husband, and I had been together for almost a year and it was time for me to meet his folks. I flew down from London to Paris, and he flew up from Nice to meet me. After a romantic dinner at his favorite restaurant in the heart of the city, we drove back late to the family home.

Everyone was asleep when we crept in that night, but the next morning I was introduced to a long series of aunts, sisters, cousins and grandparents, each welcoming and kind but each also clearly looking me over. I could read the expression on their faces: "So how come he needs to be with an English girl?"

I desperately wanted to fit in and to make myself useful. Coming from a large family myself, I quickly found a way to help with preparations for the New Year's Eve dinner planned for that evening. My French was reasonably good by then, and I had no

trouble with the vocabulary, but it was the structure of the meal itself that was hard for me to grasp. There was so much going on! All around the kitchen, different dishes were being carefully assembled. The grandmother and doyenne of the family sat in a large chair at the end of the kitchen table, overseeing the hustle and bustle and giving advice on the best way to stuff the duck or how the potatoes should be cut.

By late afternoon, all the men were outside in the cold opening oysters, while inside vegetables were chopped, and repeated trips into town produced more and more food ordered from a particular *patissier* or the favored butcher or *boulangerie*.

In the dining room I was allowed to help lay the long table, and guided by two of the cousins, I carefully positioned plates, glasses, cutlery, knife rests and white embroidered napkins for the twenty-two family members who were to sit down together a few hours later. While we concentrated on the place settings, bottles of red

Nothing beats fresh greenery from the garden to decorate for the holidays.

wine were opened and lined up on a buffet table behind us to air before the meal, while champagne and white wine were rearranged in a large refrigerator.

Excitement was mounting and around 7:00 in the evening it was time to change into our party dresses. I nervously put on a black dress and heels, hoping that I'd be neither over- nor underdressed. By the time I came back to the dining room, the champagne was open, glasses were being filled and the evening was about to begin. There was so much that was new to me that evening, and so much to take in that some details were quickly forgotten. Not concerning the food, however; this was the first time in my life that I was served an eight-course meal!

First came the oysters, huge platters of oysters placed strategically down the center of the table, with lemon quarters tied inside muslin squares placed here and there.

Plates were changed and baskets of warm toasted bread were brought out to accompany the foie gras—very rich but quite delicious. After a dry white wine for the oysters, a second glass was half-filled with a sweeter Sauternes for this course.

Next was a plate of smoked salmon, served with small triangles of toast; then plates were changed again for a hot meat pâté in a golden pastry crust, accompanied by a new wine, a red Burgundy.

I was beginning to understand why the girls at the table were taking such small >>174

ROAST DUCK WITH QUINCE AND ROOT VEGETABLES

To roast duck for a festive meal, choose your bird carefully from a reliable producer. Stuff it with your favorite stuffing: mine is a mix of sausage, bread soaked in milk, and chestnuts chopped into pieces.

Prepare the duck with the stuffing, place in a deep baking tray with a couple of sprigs of rosemary, and bake in a hot oven for around 90 minutes, depending on the weight. Baste the bird repeatedly with the juices and don't hesitate to turn the duck breast-side down to prevent the white meat becoming dry. If the juices evaporate too much during cooking, trickle water over the bird. Remember, you will want some juices at the end of the cooking for serving with a little sauce. Halfway through the cooking time, add the chestnuts to the pan, scattered around the duck.

In a separate baking dish, place four large spoonfuls of duck fat and some new potatoes cut into halves. If you can't find new potatoes, then use larger ones that have been parboiled. Keep an eye on the potatoes during cooking: you want them soft and melting inside but crispy on the outside. If you wish, you can add carrots and parsnips to this pan and cook them alongside the potatoes.

I love the combination of sweetness with festive meats, and for this recipe I peel and quarter two large quinces, sprinkle them with brown sugar, and roast them in a shallow dish in the bottom of the oven, filled with water up to one-third of their height. The water evaporates during cooking.

Once the duck is roasted, remove it from the oven, cover with aluminum foil and two or three clean tea towels and leave to rest for 10 minutes: the meat will be more tender for the wait.

While you cut the meat, drain off any juices and reheat with a large spoonful of Marsala wine to create a delicious sauce.

servings: they knew how long this was going to take! Relief from the rich food came in the shape of a tiny glass holding a scoop of apple sorbet, over which my neighbor poured a spoon of Calvados apple brandy. We were only halfway through the meal!

The main course was served—a beautiful stuffed goose, or actually two, roasted and served with chestnuts and truffles with three vegetable purées to accompany the dish. By now I felt I could hardly eat another thing, but the meal was not over.

Smaller plates were handed out and red wine glasses were refilled. A large cheese platter was passed slowly around the table, as the compared merits of each one were discussed. It dawned on me that a lot of the conversation throughout the meal was about food. Talking about the food in our plates was part of the enjoyment and the tradition: where the foie gras came from; whether the goose was as tender as last year's; or whether the Roquefort cheese was creamy enough. Everyone chimed in with their point of view, and the atmosphere around the noisy, happy table seemed light-years from any meal I had ever experienced.

After the cheese was cleared away, two log-shaped chocolate cakes, or *Bûche de Noël,* were brought out on a long, narrow plate. Apparently one had a chestnut cream filling and the other chocolate. I tasted a tiny slice of the chestnut cream cake and promised myself that in the highly unlikely event of ever feeling hungry again, I definitely needed to investigate the flavor further.

That evening was a remarkable introduction to a special and loving family. It also gave me an amazing insight into the way the French live and their singular gift for entertaining. Little could I know that this evening would be the first of many others, and that in less than a year I'd be living full time in France, embarking on a new life and discovering so much more about this country that I would make my own.

Red wine glasses echo the red roses and holly berries in the table center.

BÛCHE DE NOËL

This is the most traditional French dessert for the holidays. It can be homemade but is quite often purchased from a favorite patissier. I believe that homemade is always better, and this is my favorite recipe.

FOR THE CREAM:

2 cups (475ml) heavy whipping cream

¼ cup (2oz, or 60g) confectioners' sugar

½ cup (1 ¾oz, or 50g) cocoa

FOR THE CAKE:

1 cup (5oz, or 130g) cake flour, sifted

1 ½ teaspoon baking powder

2 eggs, room temperature

¾ cup (6oz, or 170g) granulated sugar

2 tablespoons whole milk

½ teaspoon salt

½ teaspoon vanilla extract

FOR THE CREAM:

Whip the cream to stiff peaks. Slowly add the sugar and cocoa. Refrigerate until needed. You may need more or less cocoa and confectioners' sugar depending on temperature and other circumstances. If you like to use a lot of frosting, you may want to make a double batch of this! Be prepared just in case.

FOR THE CAKE:

Preheat the oven to 375°F (190°C) and line a rectangular sheet pan with waxed paper for baking the cake. Sift together the flour and baking powder. Set aside.

Using an electric mixer, beat the eggs for 30 seconds. While mixing, pour in the sugar slowly. Continue mixing until the mixture is a pale yellow color (this is crucial to the recipe). Add the milk, salt, and vanilla. Stir to combine. Lightly fold in the dry ingredients with a spatula. Do not overmix. Transfer batter to the prepared sheet pan.

Bake for 10 to 14 minutes, or until light golden in color. When you can gently push the surface of the cake with your fingertips and watch it rise back slowly, the cake is ready.

Let cool for about 5 minutes. Prepare a second section of waxed paper to receive the cake by laying it on a clean tea towel and coating it lightly with confectioners' sugar. Turn the cake out onto the paper. Working quickly but not roughly, gently roll the paper up with the cake inside of it. Let it cool for 10 minutes and then unroll the towel.

When the cake is completely cool, fill it with the chocolate cream and roll it up again. Frost the outside completely. If the frosting starts to melt, stick it in the freezer for a while.

Take your time, and remember, this cake is supposed to look like a log! Making it at home can be challenging but fun. Decorate however you wish. If you would like to make a chocolate "bark," melt any type of chocolate and spread it thinly on a piece of parchment. Place it in the freezer until it hardens, then crack it and press it onto your cake. A dusting of confectioners' sugar creates the appearance of fresh snow. This is a time to get creative!

The staircase is decorated with fresh greenery and candles in glass holders, something we could never do when the children were little.

A heavy winter frost dusts the valley in pale white and seems to highlight every leaf and branch.

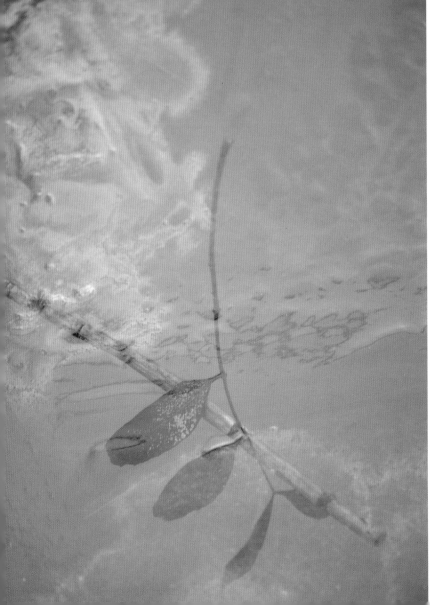

CHRISTMAS AND NEW YEAR'S

IN SILVER

Christmas doesn't have to be about red berries and traditional festive colors. Sometimes a more neutral palette feels welcome and gentler to the eye. Here white roses blend with silver ornaments with a touch of mauve added to the mix. It's as much about texture as color.

When the house is decorated for the holidays, it's a good moment to invite friends over for a glass of champagne in front of the fire. It doesn't have to be a full meal, just an early evening drink before dinner.

CHOCOLATE MOUSSE

MAKES 8 SINGLE-PORTION POTS

A tiny individual chocolate mousse is the perfect way to finish a festive meal, a touch of sweetness to accompany a coffee.

10 ounces (300g) good-quality dark
  chocolate

Generous ½ cup (5fl oz, or 15cl) cream

3 egg yolks

6 egg whites

¼ cup (1 ¾ oz, or 50g) sugar

First, heat the chocolate very, very gently, either in a microwave or in a bain-marie. Whatever you do, don't let it get too hot.

When the chocolate has just melted, add the cream one-third at a time and beat continuously with a spoon to mix everything smoothly. Add the egg yolks and beat again.

Beat the egg whites until stiff, adding the sugar little by little as you go.

Mix a spoonful of the egg whites into the chocolate cream thoroughly, then gently fold in the rest of the egg whites. Spoon the pudding into your little pots and refrigerate for up to 12 hours. Serve cold, with a little pouring chocolate if you wish, although I like them as they are.

Even the dogs enjoy the novelty of the
snow that transforms the garden and
the valley.

MIMOSA
AND LEMONS

I first lived in France as a student in the southern town of Nice. Arriving on the Cote d'Azur at the beginning of the school year in September, I was immediately struck by the beautiful light, so typical of the end of summer. There was a perfume on the air and I was immediately hooked. So began my love affair with this country and my learning curve on French living. New foods, new sounds and smells, and new friends. Every day brought its share of surprises and encounters.

The mild seasons were also a wonderful discovery. Seasonal changes have always been important to me, and as we edged through midwinter in the south and came to February, I was excited to see the light alter, becoming crisper and brighter than the soft, subtle lights of the Provençal summer.

That first winter I also discovered the Mimosa tree. From February through March, the hills behind the Cote d'Azur are covered in its bright yellow blossoms whose scent floats across the town on the breeze. The local markets are heavy with the fragrance of the bunches of cut Mimosa branches sold there, while visually the yellow of the flowers are echoed by the bright lemons that are harvested all along the coast during these late-winter months. The snap of the color feels like a wake-up call, a reminder that spring is only just around the corner: calling out to get ready but >>207

LEMON TART WITH MERINGUES

MAKES ONE 9-INCH (23CM) TART OR 6 INDIVIDUAL TARTS

This is surprisingly simple to make, and I prefer to keep the flavor as pure as possible, avoiding cream or flour in the lemon and egg mix. Make the meringues first so they can be cooling while you bake the tart.

FOR THE MERINGUES:

2 egg whites

2/3 cup (120g) fine white sugar

FOR THE TART:

1 sweet pastry crust*

3 large eggs

3 egg yolks

3/4 cup (6oz, or 170g) butter

3/4 cup (5 1/2oz, or 150g) sugar

Juice of 4 lemons

Zest of 1 lemon

Small meringues, for serving

FOR THE MERINGUES

Preheat the oven to 210°F (100°C).

Using an electric mixer, beat the egg whites in a large mixing bowl until they are firm enough to stand in stiff peaks. Slowly add half the sugar, a spoonful at a time, beating well after each addition. The egg whites will become thicker and quite shiny. Gently fold in the remaining sugar, again a spoonful at a time, until all the sugar is added and the mixture is white and smooth.

Drop or spoon small quantities of the egg white mixture onto a baking sheet lined with parchment paper, forming small rounds; you can shape these into swirls using the end of the spoon or a knife. Bake for about 70 minutes, until the meringues feel light and sound hollow when tapped underneath. Top each mini tart with a cooled meringue or place them side by side on the top of the whole tart.

FOR THE TART

Heat the oven to 350°F (180°C) and blind bake the pastry crust(s) until golden brown. Beat the eggs and yolks together.

In a saucepan, heat the butter, sugar, lemon juice and zest, along with the beaten eggs and egg yolks. Heat gently until the butter is melted, stirring and whisking all the time. You don't want the mixture to overheat because the eggs could scramble. Once the mixture has thickened enough to coat the back of a wooden spoon, remove from the heat.

Using a fine strainer, pour the hot lemon mixture through the strainer and into a bowl. You can use a spoon or a spatula to push it all through. Then pour your lemon curd into the pastry crust(s) and return to the oven for about 6 minutes. You want the curd to be just set but still quite soft. Remove from the oven and allow to cool. This tart can be eaten warm or cold.

*If making individual tarts, you will need additional pastry crust.

also to appreciate each fleeting moment of the passage from winter to spring

Although I no longer live in the south of France, I still keep a lookout for Mimosa blossoms at my local florist shops. The season is short and it's worth buying three or four bunches, enough to fill a large vase. Before adding water and arranging the flowers, I love to amplify the instant sunshine effect by filling the glass vase with lemons. We need this input of brightness at the end of our gray winter. A zest of citrus to wake us up is also welcome, especially when it comes in the shape of a little lemon tart. The sharpness of the fruit, accompanied by the sweetness of the meringue makes a wonderful dessert or teatime enticement.

There is nothing like the bright yellow of mimosa and lemons to wake us up at the end of the winter and reassure us that the spring is on its way.

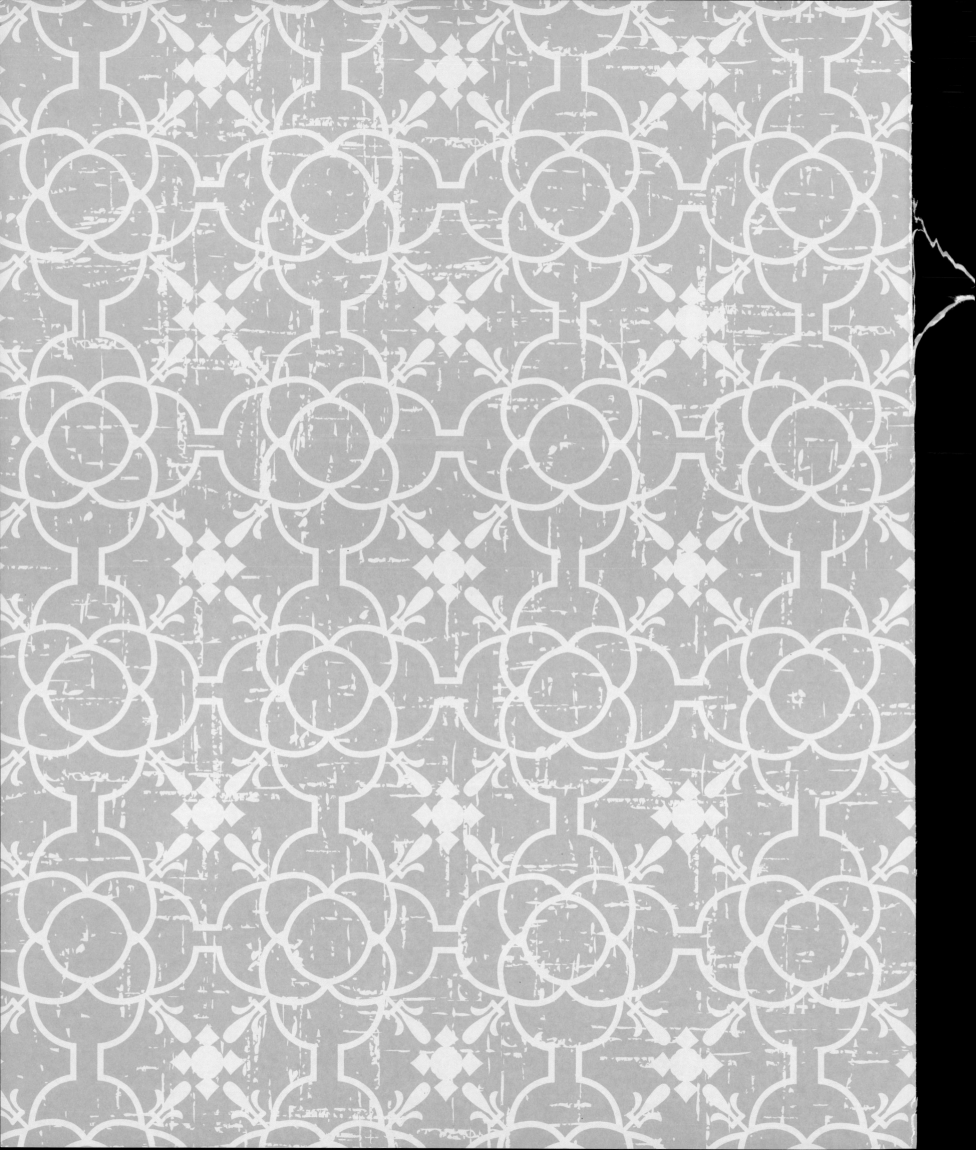